THE WEDDING BOAT

Sue Ellen Thompson

Owl Creek Press
1620 N. 45th St.
Seattle WA 98103

for Diane and Richard Adams

ACKNOWLEDGMENTS

The poems in this volume have previously appeared in the following magazines:

Connecticut Review: "Scanning the Obits," "Three Wishes," "Sunset at the Grand Canyon," "Starting Over"
Embers: "A Young Man's Body"
Great Stream Review: "The Men"
G. W. Review: "House Guests"
Negative Capability: "The Bride's Story"
New Virginia Review: "White Bath, High Window"
North Carolina Humanities: "With My Second Husband, Thinking of My First"
Northeast Magazine: "Last Sail," "Night of the Prom," "Two Women Swimming in Maine," "Second Home"
Southern Poetry Review: "Easier"
Tar River Poetry: "Quenched," "The Stranger"
The Georgia Review: "How to Tell a True Love Story"
The Louisville Review: "The Landlord"
The New Review: "Terms of Endearment," "Remembering My Parents' Sex Life"
The Sow's Ear: "Perfect," "What I Wanted"

CONTENTS

I. DESIRE'S ORBIT

The Bride's Story	8
Night of the Prom	10
April	11
Saved	12
The Landlord	14
White Bath, High Window	15
A Young Man's Body	17
Quenched	18
Reading the Poem	19
The Stranger	21
January	22
Scanning the Obits	23
Easier	24
What I Wanted	25
Learning Yoga: The Crow	27
Researching the Dictionary of Saints, Heroes and Holy People	28
Terms of Endearment	29
Remembering My Parents' Sex Life	30
How to Tell a True Love Story	32

II. THE WEDDING BOAT

Two Women Swimming in Maine	34
The American Hotel	36
Perfect	37
The Mowing	39
House Guests	40
The Men	42
Couples	43
The Wedding Boat	45
Home Decor	47
Last Sail	48
November	50

Sunset at the Grand Canyon   51
Second Home   52
With My Second Husband, Thinking of My First   54
Divorce   55
Starting Over   57
Three Wishes   58
Reunion   60

I. DESIRE'S ORBIT

The Bride's Story

I'm not the mother who dabs at the stain
above her breast to stave
off tears as the bride waves
good-by, nor am I the father whose disdain

for the boy his daughter has chosen to marry
is evident. I am not the groom
who guides her through the flume
of rice and rose-petals, who carries

her to his idling car, trailing
streamers in a foreshadowing of blood.
Her bouquet lifts into the night, then scuds
across the pavement toward an ailing

maiden aunt, wheelchair-bound,
and the crowd hangs back, chastened.
I cannot tell you what hastened
or slowed their departure, or who found

the car, wheels spinning, or what kind of fool
would mix these two occasions,
but I like to think that her evasions
were playful, that from somewhere in that cloud of tulle

she beckoned him, and would have taught
him love in the undoing
of a thousand buttons; and that misconstruing
her long look backward, he thought

he saw her resolve go slack
and swerved to avoid it. I'm not the surgeon
who unzipped her abdomen to find the burgeon
of a child in its small glazed sac,

nor am I among the wedding
guests who huddle, three days later,
at her grave. I'm not the investigator
who was last seen threading

his way through mourners to arrest the groom
for driving under the influence,
nor did I play a part in this confluence
of love and death. But I'm the one to whom

the bride has left her story:
it pulls at me like a train of lace
and wraps my nights in its fierce embrace,
a constant reminder of the transitory

joy of the wedding day, when we pretend
to choose what is already chosen
and the sweet cream of the future lies frozen
on our plates. The bride's story doesn't end

here, in the telling, any more than bed
puts an end to the tragedy of desire.
Each death ignites its own small fire,
and with this poem, I thee wed.

Night of The Prom

It's more than the passage of years,
which lowers a scrim of sadness and loss
between us and the occasion.
It begins when the car makes an arc in the driveway,
where the adults of the family are assembled
in their cameras and old spring sweaters,
watching as she alights in a cloud of hair,
bare brown shoulders pushed up
like new mountains from a sea of bluish lace.
It is not longing
that tilts and tinges the scene
until we cannot be sure who these fledglings may be;
or envy,
although it is true I never spent a night in May
beneath the crenellated awnings of a paper Camelot.
Perhaps it is how much they look alike,
with their reddish curls and ruffled white carnations,
hands locked like the branches of a tree
whose trunk, willowy and green, sways
invisibly between them.
They could be brother and sister,
a thought that comforts us,
conferring an innocence upon the evening air--
or two children playing dress-up
in a musty tux and old lace veil.
But no, it is this:
that when they pose for photographs
in the purplish dusk of the small back yard,
a crown of dogwood lights for a moment
in her hair, making these two
king and queen of a world
where to be blessed is to believe in the
choices these blossoms were sent out to make.

April

When I was seventeen and tossed about
the sky above Samoa by a cruel typhoon,
I met a boy, heartsick for the girl
he'd left behind in Adelaide.
He let me fall into a deep, pretended sleep
across his lap, and when with every lift
and fall into the spiral of the storm
our hearts were teased
into a momentary buoyancy,
I let his troubled hands trace palm trees
on my sleeping breasts. Sure,

we stayed in touch, and once or twice
embraced on city streets, at the edge
of a skyscraper's sheer glass drop.
What has all this to do
with a season that ages instantly,
or with the jonquils felled
by last night's turbulence? Just that
I flew today, a foot or two
above the infant pink magnolia,
archipelago of phlox, and found myself
blooming again in the maelstrom above
the lawn's rough adolescence, between
two continents, alive.

Saved

In college I was plucked right off the student union
    terrace
by a boy who looked as though he'd be a movie star
some day. He had a skier's easy grace
and the kind of shoulders Nordic women weep for

when they knit. Cursing with facility in Swedish,
he'd kick the covers to the floor each time I said
I wasn't ready. One Sunday afternoon
I waited for him in the library, my long hair brushed

and fanned across my back. I saw him park his car
and followed him, carrying my books before me
like a shield. Crouched in the violet shadows
cast by the college chapel, I saw his light go on

then off again, the shape of him behind the curtains
shrugging off his shirt. That simple motion
was to me desire as I had not yet known it:
To think of him in that relation to his clothes,

that he could cast them off and simply be
himself, moving through the dormitory's heated air
to take a book down, or to lie across the bed
with arms upraised, the skin there white

as mountains mapped with bluish trails.
I crept out from my hiding place and went
to him, I knocked and waited, knocked again
and saw, beyond the shoulder of his robe,

an Oriental girl cross-legged in the spiral of a sheet.
Last night I saw him on t.v. again.
He played a doctor who had killed his partner
so he'd have the practice and his partner's wife.

His face at forty-two was coppery and smooth,
his hair the glossy pewter of a good fur coat.
As they led him from the courtroom
in his well-pressed suit, he turned

12

and looked at me across that same betraying shoulder,
turned his perfect grown man's head,
eyes rimmed with longing and regret.
I knew then I'd saved myself

by watching from the shadows, saved myself
for this moment, worth that look and more.

The Landlord

Feigning sleep in his lawnchair on the front stoop
of my first apartment, he has made it all
but impossible for me to pass. I'm twenty-two,
he's in his forties--some would call

him a devoted husband, a God-
fearing man, with his Amish beard
and eyes the color of fresh-turned sod.
Not yet having learned to fear

a man for what he might do, I speak
to him long and politely enough to get by.
The next morning I oversleep
and awake feverish, nightgown stuck to my thighs

as I stumble downstairs to put out the trash.
I hear the slow grind of a doorknob, and later
a sound at the foot of the stairs like an animal scratch.
He calls my name, and it rises like water

through the oil of my fevered half-sleep.
He says his wife has cancer, since she's been sick
she's closeted herself from him, as if to keep
her dying secret--that he'd be quick

and gentle, and tell no one. Would I just come
to the top of the stairs and let him look
at me? When I do, he exhales like some
poor crushed animal, and it takes what it took

Eve to say Yes for me to say No.
From the lace of my hem to the backlit hall,
he takes me in, slower than slow,
he drinks me down, ice and all.

White Bath, High Window

For the cat, it's the eiderdown flung
in the corner on laundry day;
for the baby, it's all in the thumb,
while with the other nine fingers he plays

his blanket like a clarinet; and for my dead
uncle it was the plush red seat
of the concert hall, where he'd nod his head
as if to show that he found the beat

of quartet or partita entirely reasonable.
For my mother it was the ironing board
where she pressed collars double
and pondered her lot over cord-

uroy seams and the nasty box pleats
of our jumpers. If for each
of us there is a place of retreat,
a place we reflect on ourselves, where we reach

some irreducible knowledge of all that we know,
then for me it's the porcelain couch of my dreams,
the tub that I bathed in a decade ago:
deep and pacific, upholstered in steam

with a ceiling that vaulted in high gothic style;
stone walls, tile floor, and near the top
of the vault a window through which sunlight spiralled
on cold autumn mornings, and moonlight dropped

like a robe on clear evenings. It was there,
having waited all night for a man to appear
as arranged, for the scuttle of footsteps on the stair,
that I drew the last bath of my thirtieth year.

It was that futile night, submerged to the ears
in my favorite element, that I heard
my heart's muffled iambic, clear
as the pulse of a ship. And what stirred

in me then is what stirs in me now:
a love that while it may not go beyond
the love of men, somehow
contains it, the way a pond

is contained by the earth around it and seems
more significant simply for being so small
and unnavigable. If being a poet means
being a woman with something to fall

back on, something encompassing, something that
      scans,
if imperfectly, true to our imperfect selves,
then this is the place where my life began:
Lincoln College at Oxford, Room 5, Stairway 12.

A Young Man's Body

is the tree I climbed as a child,
to look back
on the house where I lived,
shimmering
in the August heat.
It is the body I house
within my own,
weighted now
by sheds and porticoes,
its center chimney hidden
by a closet,
warm to the touch
in winter.

If I notice you
it is because
I am thinking of
my brothers
in their football prime,
their shoulders roofed in pads
from which their loose shirts
flapped like awnings.
If I look at you
too long
it is because
I am in love with
architecture, and the building
is so beautiful
before the ground is
broken.

Quenched

He had eyes the color of my first iced tea
in the Australian outback, that day in '65
the station owner's wife, who'd lived once in America,
saw the heat-stunned students
raising a reddish column of dust
as they trekked back from the shearing shed
and reappeared with seven glasses chiming on a tray.
Sometimes it comes upon you like a thirst
as you stumble through a weekday's parched routine,
rising to your lips in a thin foam you can almost taste:
the first kiss with its lemon bite, the grainy
residue of sweetness with the last.

Afterwards, the taut blond meadow of his belly
rose and fell in dappled light.
Some part of me already gathered
clothes from branches where I'd flung them,
inventoried earrings, purse, my watch
and all the hours I'd have to justify.
I held him by his teacup chin
and watched the contents of our meeting
vanish in the reflex of a swallow,
the sweat along his porcelain brow receding
to a glaze and then to simple skin
as he rose on his thin white legs and dressed.

Reading The Poem

I look at him across the room
when he's not looking: the poem

in his tight blue jeans
and shapeless sweater, I

in my single strand of pearls.
He's younger than I thought

and far more handsome: flecks
of pure green verb leap in his eyes.

I introduce myself--an erstwhile
wife and mother, on her own tonight

and looking to reclaim her lost
intelligence. We start out

slowly, the poem and I, aware
we may not spend more

than this brief evening
together. He tells the story

of his brother's drowning,
and something in the way he does

this, all the while folding paper napkins
into pale pink swans, well,

that impresses me. By evening's end
he's got his fingers in my neck-curls,

he walks me to my car
under spring's first scattering

of stars. He's telling me
how difficult it was to pull his brother

from the water, how he dropped him
in the shallows, had to press

the steaming cup of his mouth
against his brother's bluish lips.

Just as I am thinking
I could do that, he turns

and winds a fist in my hair,
bending the sure strong arc

of his body over my trembling
own. But instead of the rough kiss

I'm expecting, the kind of kiss
that women like to read about,

the poem turns and takes
the pavement with him, he

turns and leaves me falling, falling
into the place where he has been.

The Stranger

This handsome man, divorced, arrives in town
and all of us are mad for him, straining from behind
our steering wheels to catch a glimpse. He is there
at every summer party, silver-templed and impeccable,
talking business with our husbands,
wrapped in faint cocoons of aftershave and scotch.
I've watched him fix a woman with his cobalt stare
from fifteen yards, I've seen her try to pull away
from that, to twist her shoulders toward another
        conversation
while her head is still as the head of a marionette,
the rest of her body lifting and floating
away. Any one of us would leave with him tomorrow
if he asked us, if he turned his burnished face in our
        direction.
But he keeps us waiting, never guessing how
this fans our small desire:

                        All those years
of waiting for the station wagon to appear
in the pool of streetlight at the corner, for it to clear
the driveway's lip, curving down to the garage,
then listening for footsteps heavy on the cellar stairs.
For this is how they enter you,
beginning in the dark where love is made
and moving up through laundry, toys,
the hooks where coats are sloughed like skins.
My father always paused a few steps from the top,
afraid the door might suddenly explode on him,
his children's faces brighter than a bulb.
He'd stand there jingling his car keys in the darkness,
breathing in the concrete air, afraid
of what love might do to him.

January

The way age has laid
its silver at your temples,
drawn its finest lines
from nose to chin;
the way you hold your head
like a skyline in winter,
perpendicular to the light;
the way your clothes fit,
impervious as fur;
the way you stand
at the entrance to yourself,
forbidding all travellers by sea
is the way January stands
at the opening of the year,
warning us that its days
are candescent but cold,
cold and brief
in their angled arc across the sky,
that the colors it casts are impossible
in their perfection, colors
about which nothing can be said--
except what a friend once said:
that she just liked to look at you,
that it made her feel like a man.

Scanning the Obits

What woman hasn't scudded through a stop
light, the better to observe
the driver in the car ahead, or swerved
to follow a near-stranger, the one who dropped

his lighter on the street, and finally bringing
flame and cigarette together, caught her eye
and held it, burning, for a moment? Why
shouldn't she go home singing

a little tune of what-might-be? And why
not be consumed for months to follow
by lust for details of his ordinary life?
And what if she should choose to wallow

in the wake of his indifference, to dispense
her life into the dark container of his own,
to languish unrequited, in a sense
invisible? The passionate among us have always known

desire's orbit to be elliptic. Why else would I,
like crows who sweep the landscape under waning
autumn's low penumbral sky,
be scanning the obituaries, feigning

nonchalance, waiting for the death
of one whose son did this to me?
What else could her last breath
mean but the opportunity to see

each other at the funeral, where he'll
be caught in sorrow's shade, while
I am radiant in black? The gods who wield
the orrery of sex will no doubt smile

as he racks his griefstruck brain to place
me. I'll cast my kindled eye on his pale face
and, in the midst of death, I'll be the one
who makes him walk the gossamer he's spun.

Easier

to take the skin from an orange,
to see its fragrance like a protest rise
a little way, then fall back,

to feel its acid seep
into the small geography winter etches
into fingers, to bite headlong

into that bittersweet profusion of flesh and rind.
Easier to lie awake in the cavernous hours,
making dreams out of nothing

but the sheerest, most willed desire--
the kind of dreams where the man is beautiful
but dumb, he *does not speak,*

so overwhelmed is he by your willingness
to sink to his level. Easier
to drive through snakeskin streets

with the elaborate care of the newly drunk,
to see a public telephone gleaming
like a gold tooth in the night's dark leer,

to enter it and call someone you might have married once
in California--where it is barely bedtime,
where none of this has happened yet--

than to say No to the man who stands here,
hands curling and uncurling
in the space between his hips and yours,

watching you undress
this tight-skinned orange
with the passionate efficiency of a wife.

What I Wanted

A dress, when I was young,
one of those floor-length ectomorphs that hung
in the "Better Dresses" section of J. M. Towne's,

of palest aqua crepe, scooped low
and empire-waisted, an underinflated bow
that floated, breast-like, just below

where my breasts would be moored.
And later, in my twenties, a job as editor
I wanted so badly I could feel the yaw

and pitch of the office chair, which fit
my ass the way a wallet fits
a man's (an ergonomic

dream!), the sunlight measuring
its bars of shade against the cream
formica desktop, coffee and the reassuring din

of phones and typewriters. I got that job,
its venal cast of characters, the squabbling
over office space and money, the S.O.B.

of a boss who sent me with my summa cum laude
master's degree in English (but a Ph.D.
in feminine compliance) to buy lingerie

for his wife's birthday, whose monstrous thighs
touched mine when he whispered, *What's your size?*
I got the dress, too, in a daze

of daughterly gratitude, but wore it only
once, and now it hangs alone
in the cedar closet, a kind of old age home

for dresses. And what does this portend
for you--my princely, my resplendent friend
in the rough black sweater and scudding wind,

slipping into foul weather gear
and stepping off the dock as if it were
a dais, sweeping out to sea in a blur

of pennants waving? Just that I'm yours,
eternal ingenue in period dress,
perpetual apprentice to imagined bliss,

bearing gifts to speed you in your race:
peach and aqua nylon, bows, stretch lace,
anything to make the old mistakes.

Learning Yoga: the Crow

Squat on the mat and plant
your hands before you. Lean
forward slightly, pressing your elbows
into your knees and try to imagine
supporting your entire weight,
the way a bird does, on two
thin wrists.
Splay your fingers,
give each one time to accept
its fragment of responsibility.
You must trust the arms that taper earthward
from the fullness of the skies.
You must lean
into the posture, letting your weight
seek out that much-sought-after place they call
the center.
With a deep breath let your body,
crouched as if to flee, come forward--
as if drawn to the lip of something, as if unable to resist
that one swift look into the already known.
Now tilt a little further forward
until your feet have left the ground
without your exactly meaning them to, as if
you were in love. Now stay
that way.

Researching the Dictionary of Saints, Heroes and Holy People

I love this work, the xeroxed indices
of sourcebooks stacked
like freshly ironed sheets,
and trapped within their folds
the undiluted fragrance
of a chemical ink,
as piercingly unsweet
as semen. When has a man's name
lingered and caroused like these--
Agastya, Uthman ibn
al-Kattab, Shen-shiu,
the Venerable Bede?
Speed-reading texts the way
one scans a lover's body
in that hushed first sighting,
drawing back the sheets,
I've learned to let my eye
take charge, the way a young pianist
learns to trust her hands
when seeking out a chord.
My body in a breathless curve
above the handsomely bound page
of an encyclopedia, one finger
slipping through the words
as if through chest-hairs,
how can I not regard
this work as sexual,
when I find your name
among the names of those
who must have pleased
a woman once?

Terms of Endearment

Sweet biscuit of my life,
I've been thinking of your smile
and how I'd steal a little bite
of it if you were here; of the delights

I've known in the alleyway between
the whitewashed storefronts of your teeth;
of how I've pressed one smithereen
after another of mille-feuille, mousseline

of late-night conversation upon your lips,
forever poised at the brink of kissdom,
their slightest sigh enough to lift
a tableskirt. Perfectest pumpkin

in the patch, your heft on mine
is what I crave, your brows so fine
I could not carve them with a steak knife.
You have the acorn eyes

of the football season, the ass
of an autumn afternoon, of boys en masse
in soccer shorts. Yours is the vast
contained candescence of a Titian under glass,

it is the gold leaf laid
by February sun, the lemonade's
pale wash in August. Should you fade,
like sun on windowsills crocheted

with shadow, then suddenly gone dark,
your face will leave its watermark
upon this page, which is already part
of love's confection, our little work of art.

Remembering My Parents' Sex Life

They danced in the kitchen
while supper was on--

bodies pressed, Glen Miller,
all six burners on the old Caloric

flicking their skirts of flame,
the tuneless buzz

of my father's hummed accompaniment
like an insect trapped

beneath the music--
pure interlude, six children

in ten years. A pinch,
a slap, flesh resonating

its applause,
a dip and sweep

among the tapping pot-lids,
scattered cats and chairs.

They showered late at night--
disappeared and reappeared

in full nocturnal dress.
No bleating springs,

no sharp intake of breath
and never anything

above the flannel sheets
but one head breathing sleep

into the other's nape.
I never saw my father

naked and am grateful now
for that, grateful

that I came into my knowledge
innocent and late,

that someone had to teach me
everything except the music

which I danced to,
when my time came,

as if born to it
in all that steam and clatter.

How to Tell a True Love Story

Say he pulled her face roughly to his,
the way he once grasped a coconut

on the black sand beach, pausing to take
its sweetness in first through the eyes;

or say he pulled her down like a rare book,
his face dissolving in wonder

as he fingered the leaves of her smile.
We will bring our own urgencies to the scene.

Put some obstacle in the way of their lovemaking:
have her wearing those tapered jeans

he must pick at her heels to remove;
or let their bodies impede,

his elbow snagging a silken breast,
her teeth meeting his in a kiss

that clacks like bone. Let them fail
to get it right, so there will be something unfinished

between them, something that blights
the small green fruit of their meeting

and fades into correspondence. Then let
their correspondence drop off,

a misunderstanding, a failure of passion
or nerve. But end where love

as I would have you tell it ends,
with him opening the door to the retreating light

and her falling without seeing where she is going,
or who it is that trembles there above her.

II. THE WEDDING BOAT

Two Women Swimming in Maine

The breast stroke must have been
a woman's invention, its sweet economy
of motion, the mechanism out of sight

and nothing to disturb the water's surface calm
but the head in its diurnal bob
from sleep to wakefulness. We're swimming,

naked, in an element more solid
than liquid, of a color so distinct
from any other green I've known

I won't let myself turn back
until I've named it. With our arms,
we part and then embrace

the tide that swells the narrow cove
at dawn and leaves it, six hours later,
simmering in clam-muck.

There's the grassy point where,
eighteen years ago, I brought my college boyfriend
long before he was your husband;

where we left him shivering on the beach
to swim in those miraculous bikinis
we'd bought in Damariscotta--

stuffed in plastic tubes like wands,
transparent in the water. Now our skin
repeats this magic, vanishing

in the green opacity a foot below the surface.
If I were inclined to break
this gem-like silence,

I might confess I never loved him
the way you did. And you might say
that I'd become too much the poet,

stroking out instinctively to gain some distance.
Who would have thought that you and I,
of all our friends, would swim

the epidermis, eighteen summers trailing
in our wake? But if you're right
about me, that explains

why we can share the swimmer's cadence:
Because it's given me the words to frame
our common element, like jade illumined from below.

The American Hotel

Ten years ago we said *Expense be damned*
but now we're looking hard at the price of a nightcap
in this, the guidebook still proclaims,
the best hotel in Amsterdam.

The third chair's reupholstered now by Peter,
our newly minted friend who leaned,
amid the spicey shufflings of an otherwise routine
rijstoffel, to ask, "Are you monogamous?"

Three floors up, the room they gave us then
quivers with amusement from its turned-down twins.
But funny, isn't it, that this is all we can remember:
how the Flemish maid looked quizzical

as we gesticulated *honey-moon.* Once more
our hopes for ease in life are dashed
as Peter slips me not the hundred guilder note
I reached for but a business card

with private P.O. box, it says in pencil,
for billets-doux. As if I didn't know.
Now we've space and time and all, it seems,
but money as we spill out to the Leidseplein,

so brightly lit and raucous with the habits of the young.
Peter wants to split a cab and thanks, but no--
we'll amble arm-in-arm
back to the grim Hotel Olschewski,

saying little in our separate but contented states
about the past, suddenly so near it seems
affordable, like the aging whore who, raked
by reddish light, beckons from a window.

PERFECT

Couples, some with children, flood
the studded hillside with its grid
of spruce and fir. Some are armed

with saws to cut their trees down early--
tags have been switched by the worldly
among us, and Christmas is hardly

the time to take up trust,
with signs in all the parking lots
reminding us that we must lock

our valuables inside. As usual,
you're eager to be done with it and pull
aside the first remotely conical

shrub you find. But I've got
the saw, and simply saunter on
as if you were a tree yourself, and far

from perfect. See Jack and Jill,
who came with us, head up the hill
in silence? Last night she told

me he was seeing someone else and hasn't
touched her in six months. Isn't
it enough to break your heart (and wasn't

their marriage too perfect to be true?)?
Instead of the plump blue spruce
you hold up a spikey, goose-

necked pine. No no,
it will not do.
Why must you

be so quick to settle for less than what
could be ours? And what
does it say about the two of us

and our flawed companions on this hunt
that we seek the perfect form in nature
we can't quite manufacture

on our own by framing
a tent above our children, or by leaning
toward each other, warming

the bitter air that separates
the long-married? If earth is the base
and we're the sides, then your face

and mine together form a vertex
when we agree, be it sex
or aesthetics. Don't let me wax

geometric, it was my only C
in high school. Forget the other trees.
In your arms, I'm the perfect isoceles.

The Mowing

You would have undone everything:
the apples gathered, bushes sculpted
into boxcars, silken grass
that let itself be cut in perfect stripes,
the cat asleep in her summerhouse
beneath the dense forsythia
as you moved closer.

But when I heard you cry out--
when you brought her to me
in your outstretched arms,
her small head lowered, dark half peeled
and crimson as a plum--

I knew the season of our innocent routine
had ended, comforts of the house
and yard, summer's gauze
stripped violently away.

That night we lay like two boats
restless at their moorings,
veils of moisture gathering
where we touched.
And while we labored, palm on palm,
to coil and stow the day's events,

suddenly I was at your back,
all tooth and claw
and ravenous to have it all--
the green, the fear, the salt, the blood--
the smell and taste
of my living, breathing husband.

House Guests

This is the room where they sleep:
the naval architect from Göteborg,
the British art historian
with his sturdy Scottish mistress,
the archivist from Dublin
and the underwater archaeologist from Sydney
with his golden crest of hair.
This is where they lay their suitcases,
filling them with t-shirts, baseball caps
and posters of the last American whaleship
shrouded in autumn's stagey fog.
I fix their eggs the only way I know,
my husband takes them off to work with him
and sets them loose on the museum grounds,
where they browse among the ships
and seine boats, sandbaggers and sharpies.
With their photographs of Ulla,
Veryan, Finola, Marianne
and children whose ceramic cheeks
are daubed with their country's
own peculiar pink, they bring us
books about the Irish Sea,
the history of the Hanseatic cog,
Tresco's figureheads and excavations of the Zuider
Zee, beneath whose polder sleep a thousand ships
preserved in mud and farmland.

There was a curator from Amsterdam
whose wife had died the year before,
leaving him with two young boys.
He had the inclined shoulders,
the downcast eyes of a man
who might at any moment stoop
to lift a fleck of pattern from the rug,
and when he walked he laced his hands
behind his back like wings.
When I pushed his door ajar to wake him
and saw the clothes he'd stacked and folded neatly
in her memory, should I have made the crossing from

my country to his own,
slipping beneath the waves of his sleep
and letting him think what he might
of American wives? He left us
a book on sextants, he ate his breakfast
and thanked us, refusing a ride
to the station and walking there
with his arms pinned to his sides
by luggage, like a man determined
to be home by dark.

The Men

The first warm day of spring, the men of my town
peek out from under their dry winter roofs,
they stretch their legs
like legs that have been asleep a long time,
they rub their eyes and squint at me
as if I'd broken their sleep with my spade.
All winter they've been curled in the earth
with their children and wives,
they've gone about their work underground,
like moles tunneling in the dark.
Now they emerge from their offices
sniffing the first lush harvest of grass,
the green skirt of light that falls from the trees
and whispers along their necks.
There in the sun
they feel the power of their sex returning,
they turn and turn their heads in the sun
until their suits turn iridescent
like the hard beautiful shells of beetles.
What am I then
but the slow green leaf
unfurling, the surface
on which they reinvent themselves
and the color on which they feed?
One presses the upper part of his arm
against my breast
as he lifts his golden glass to toast the season.
Another makes the silver in his pocket sing,
he rubs my thigh
with a quarter through the cloth,
thinking of how it shines there in his body's closet,
like a child thinking what it will buy.

Couples

As a blond older sister stands
porcelain in her wedding gown
above the mantelpiece,

her countenance telling us
not to strive for beauty or love,
she has attained them for all of us,

you and your husband always stood apart
from those who wobbled and broke
in the wake of your example.

When you tell me
he didn't work late last night,
that you followed him in the early dark,

driving like a madwoman
to keep him in sight,
that you saw him

pull up to a low blue house
leaping from the car
as a younger man might

to a woman who stood
in a shaft of light
from the kitchen,

wrapped in a robe
the color of spring flesh,
it is as if my sister

had just stepped down
from the mantel,
unhinged that frangible

dress at the shoulders
and let it fall to the floor
like the dress of a paper doll.

It is as if she turned
from the photographer
and his globes of light,

the bow of her smile unraveling
in a dark ribbon of fear,
hair falling down her back

like a prayer--
and took me
by my bridesmaid's shoulders

still cased in the pale taffeta
of my late teens
and said to me,

*It's not what you think.
I'm alone most nights and
sometimes he hurts me.*

The Wedding Boat

Last weekend, at the wedding of a friend,
I saw a man whose face could send
my heart skittering down
the polished stair of longing;
a man I might have loved once,
had he chosen to befriend me.
Skinny dipping off the bridal barge,
night's sequined shawl reflected
in the harbor's watered silk,
I thought I saw his darkened form
weaving through the shadows
of all those thrashing limbs
like an eel through eelgrass.
Giddy with champagne,
I swam in circles, mistaking profiles
left and right until my husband
hauled me up, gasping,
and wrapped me in his jacket
on the milk-white deck. The boat

returned to shore. As slim bare legs
and shirt-tailed torsos clambered upward,
one man turned (as if on bearings,
as if on cue!)--one laser glance
of mute acknowledgment.
Later, as the party loosened
by the lawn's dark edge, his wife
(the German Shepherd-eyed biologist)
came sniffing for an introduction.
We talked of custom cabinets, private schools,
fillo dough and water views,
disguising our professions in the way
that women do. I turned to leave.
She caught my arm,
where just above the sleeve's pale mouth
I felt her nails like canines pierce
the silk. Hair on fire
in the streetlight, cheeks still burnished
by the sun but downy,
like a child's, she might have had me

by the throat as she hissed
her hoarse command: *You keep
your eyes off my husband, understand?*

Home Decor

It was below the Cutty Sark, a pub in Greenwich,
where the barges sniff their way
up the chocolate path of the Thames;

where, against a sea wall coppered by the sun,
the man whose car is shrinking from my driveway,
whose kiss lies dry upon my cheek,

pulled a bag of chips from his pocket,
set two amber mugs of beer upon the slate
and said, "We'll get married then."

All of England pinched to this one scene
repeated through the years, its marbled breath
of fuel and water, grease on newsprint, beer--

no larger than the wharfside scene
in this book of reproduction wallcoverings,
on which it seems my life must now depend.

Exotic birds on branches,
a spiral of flowers in imitation of Versailles,
my choices are confined to stripes

or the miniature repetitions of small town life.
In the pages of this fragrant book I see,
the way one sees one's face by glimpses

in the mirror of a passing train,
my life is small, smaller
than a window pane.

Last Sail

This is the last
sail of the season. It is clear

from the way
the clouds gather force

and force their way
across the sky,

clear from the silence
you assume at the tiller

that this is the kind of chill
that settles in and stays there

for the season.
Our daughter fills the air

with splashes, knock-
knock jokes and screams that sound

like wind
winding through the shrouds.

We ought to go
to that funeral, I say.

She was a friend,
and to find her husband

cold on the kitchen floor like that.
I find all this enough to make me want

to knock that tiller
from your hands and jibing, knock

you senseless.
But this is not the way we do things

in New England,
where the weather comes upon us

like a war
we know is wrong,

where we are accustomed
to certain seasons of hardship.

Which is why
when you say nothing, I say nothing.

November

That tall Texan who herds
his '57 Thunderbird
into the scrub of my driveway
at five past eight each morning,
does a rhumba with his coffee cup,
then ushers my skinny daughter in
beside his buxom own
would call this leafless waste
a season of glorious neglect.
Everything about his world
is oversize, and he expands
to fill it, shouting *Hello gorgeous!*
to my sweat ensemble or flapping robe,
and *Let me help you with that, darlin'*
if I'm wrestling with firewood.

Why should his ranch-size cheeriness
embitter me, already fitted out
for winter with my native brand
of thin-lipped resignation?
Only a Yankee understands
November's parsimonious light,
the economy of speech
between a husband and his wife
who may have loved
extravagantly in darkness.

Sunset at the Grand Canyon

The light, I learned, was everything--
the way it hauled itself

up from the canyon floor at sunset,
leafing the palisades with gold.

It could turn the postcard
of a distant monolith to film--

leaping, almost speaking with color.
Or it could turn

on its heel, leaving its striated sheets
of landscape stacked against the rim

like flats after the play has closed.
The single cloudy day of our vacation

we argued over nothing and watched
our not-quite-teenage girl grow sullen,

hurling herself repeatedly against
the false blue light of the pool.

If there had been sun, we might have seen
the slightest swelling of a breast

beneath her pale green suit. Instead,
the sky grew dark, released some rain

and still we sat there watching
from the silence of our chairs,

while like a bird she
rose, and preened, and disappeared.

Second Home

Housewives love November, before the snow
lays down its fake white fur, before the thaw

trudges in with its muddy boots.
Just beyond the ridge that blocks our view

the mountains are lined up against the sky,
each peak paler and more beckoning

with distance. Here in the yard,
the trees pitch in the early dusk,

wrapped in their thin black coats
and shivering theatrically.

I help my husband move crushed granite,
stippled pink and gray, into a drainage ditch,

thinking of coral beaches, thinking of the day
this boggy northern plot will catch the sun.

My husband, back hurting, thinks only of ice dams,
spring floods, paint cans tipped and floating

in the basement. But as the sun
splinters through clouds for one brief moment

before slipping into its mountain envelope,
and as the trees reach up with knitted fingers

to catch their day's iota of warmth,
I can't help laying my shovel aside

and exclaiming at the beauty of it all,
the lawn swept clean by weeks of wind

and washed in sudden light. My husband,
angry at everyone today, responds

this is the coldest, darkest place on earth,
he'll never understand why I wanted this house,

its useless scrawl of poplar woods,
its muddy cellar and chill, wet drafts.

For what we've put into this place
we could have had two weeks a year in Florida

for life, no yard. I lean on my shovel
and watch the light languish and fall,

I see the trees pulling back into themselves
and I forgive him, because he doesn't know

what it feels like to be shedding something,
because he doesn't know what I'll become.

With My Second Husband, Thinking of My First

He knew light and how to bend it.
He could hold a glass of rum
up to the milky winter sky
and turn the kitchen autumn.

He bought me silks whose colors lay
like filtered lamplight on my skin.
I danced upon my crystal stem
until the room turned scarlet.

He drank too much, but he was young,
his face still luminous with years unspent,
with late nights tossed in twisted sheets,
with morning's ravenous argument,

his body always six months shy
of spoiling. To my Tantalus he played
the rising water, ripened peach. I can't deny
I dreamed of him long after he was gone,

I'd see him slinking down the driveway
in his profligate black car, his bike
and skis and all his treasures on a rack
while you lay bearded, patient, as unlike

him as any man could be--
or that I'm thinking of him now, your hand
upon our ripening daughter as we stand
before the ancient cider press like pilgrims

paying homage to the fall. We watch the pulp
pour down the chute until it's spread
in layers between burlap-covered frames.
The generator clears its throat and bends its head

to the task, bearing down like truth
upon the flesh of those who were betrayed,
pressing sweetness from the bruised and bitter,
pressing it right through the light of day.

Divorce

for Betsey

We walk through rooms you once loved
for the way they embraced the light--
the livingroom like a widow now

without its worn sofa covered in crumbs;
the music room an abandoned dream,
your son having long ago shown his preference

for sports and video games. On the piano
a photograph of the six of us,
perched in two perfect triangles above Squam Lake:

mother, father, mother, father,
child. Upstairs, we marvel at the bedroom walls,
still unfinished after 14 years,

their insulation all you thought you needed
to keep winter out. I've brought you a picnic,
but the movers haven't finished

and our kids are having the last of their fun
in the half-filled van.
So we eat it all in the hot, bare kitchen,

drinking wine, my voice like a stream
catching on everything
but you, dry-eyed, looking ahead.

The children scatter shredded lettuce everywhere
and I bend to pick it up but you stop me,
saying you've cleaned this house for the last time,

it's Jack's problem now.
Afterward, we all go out for ice cream,
which melts quickly in the heat from the parking lot.

Your son and my daughter,
friends since nursery school,
kick a soda can back and forth

and say good-bye, wrestling a little
on the grass. We embrace the way women
hardly ever embrace, our breasts

dovetailing, and you thank me for everything,
for being your friend these past eight years,
for the supper, the wine.

I stand there like the sailor's wife,
watching you, our children's childhood, the car,
the ice cream--everything getting smaller.

Starting Over

Seven months later you rise
before dawn and walk in the April air,
which is raw as a fish is raw,
full of the sea's cold, wet harvest.

The darkness hangs like a curtain of weed,
you punch at it with your elbows and fists,
walking the way a woman walks
who's put her husband behind her.

Past the season's first brave boats,
their masts strummed by halyards,
summer's old song; past the houses
just barely lit, a father spooning light

into his child's mouth--until the sky
is slit open, another day spills into spring
and you realize it's all accidental:
the way the birds lace the air with song,

the intoxicant air with its whiff of salt and rain.
More than three miles you walk
before the past catches up with you
and the season is stilled,

daffodils stopped
in their proud, ridiculous tracks
as if they thought they could pick up their crowns
and start over.

Three Wishes

I.

To be an Olympic ski jumper,
springing lightly on my haunches
at the top, a brightly colored spill
of thousands silent in the snow
awaiting my descent. The long
swift drop, the no-turning-back of it,
then flight: my body
leaning out to touch the fear
that is the spectator's native tongue.

II.

To spend one bottomless summer
on the shale-strewn shores
of Lake Champlain, hunkered
in the fragrance of the pines,
spinning the lakebottom's silvery muck
into little pots and ashtrays.
Each fistful of the stuff is better
than the last--less pebbly
and more silken as it slips
between my palm and fingers--
until it seems there is nothing
I cannot make from it.

III.

No more friends divorcing,
the babies in their strollers pushed forever
up Baptist Hill, the older ones jostling for position
on the soccer field. To pause here
in the midst of our lives, to take
what we have and spread it in our palms
like fragments of shell, to notice how the days
turn opalescent at the edge of loss.
All of us in the houses we first chose

upon coming here, the remainder
of my mornings in this chair, pen poised
in wonder at the livingroom's mid-morning
still life: a daughter's silken face framed
on the piano, a cat extended
on the snowy sofa, tea.

Reunion

Twenty years later, you are standing with her again
on the same green bedspread of lawn,
your old dorm like a painted backdrop,
her room winking its single eye
further back, behind a scrim of lilacs.
Two kids who've never known anything
but the long walk up chapel hill at sunset,
which settles now like a silk scarf
on the bunched shoulders of the Adirondacks.

The same prim mouth and tilted nose,
that halo of hair gone darker but not yet gray,
she has aged in the way all of us would wish to age,
her smile set deeper in her face,
her skin a tawny linen lined with pink
from the California sun.
A boy who's young enough to be our child
yells *Class of '70!* and like the gentle bovines we've
      become,
we amble to our place in the procession,
your hand lightly grazing her waist and I,
your wife, just a few steps behind.

But I'm not your wife yet--
not when we pass the fraternity house
where I found you drunk one Saturday night;
not when you tell me you caught her in bed
with a 25-year-old freshman,
his back already scarred from Viet Nam;
and not, finally, when I drag you out
in the sub-zero air and force you to walk with me,
the campus quiet as a drawn sheet,
inarticulate with snow.

This tree forms the lintel we all passed under
the day we left Vermont, and I hang back now
to let the two of you enter its shade together,
your heads bowed low in conversation.
I want to take my ring and close her hand around it,
tell her she is beautiful and will be happy.

I want the girl I was then to step back from the porchlight,
clutching her books to her chest,
to wait in the shadows while the two of you
continue your motionless kiss.

For this is the way we enter the past,
giving up all we claim to have won
and letting what's lost step forward.
Someone I should recognize but don't,
his blue eyes buried in the rumpled laundry of his face,
touches my arm, says
Isn't that Kathy and Stu?
Something that is not love swells
in me like love, and all I can do is say
Yes and give you back.

Sue Ellen Thompson is the author of a previous collection of poems, *This Body of Silk*, which won the 1986 Samuel French Morse Prize and was published by Northeastern University Press.